MW01290064

# The Second Collection

## Thoughts And Other Writings

Robert Brault

## Books by Robert Brault

*Round Up The Usual Subjects*

*The Second Collection*

~~~

*For Joan*
*My Wife, Partner and Soulmate*

*One day, in your search for happiness, you find*
*a partner by your side, and you realize that*
*your happiness has come to help you search.*

~~~

The Second Collection © 2015 by Robert Brault.

All writings in this book are the original work of the author, who retains sole copyright..

Robert Brault is a Connecticut free-lance writer who has contributed to newspapers and periodicals in the USA since 1961. His work appears in many published anthologies and has been quoted widely on the internet

Robert Brault is quoted several hundred times each day on Twitter.   These quotes comprise a realtime stream viewable by linking to **https://twitter.com/search?q=Robert% 20Brault&src=tyah&vertical=default&f=tweets**
.

The author welcomes reader comments at his website, **The New Robert Brault Reader (rbrault.blogspot.com)** and his email address, **bobbrault@att.net**.

Front Cover: "*Garlic, Apples and Grapes*", pastel by Joan Brault

ISBN-13:  978-1511929547
ISBN-10:  1511929545

# Author's Note

I want to underscore the fact that all writings in this book are original .

Some may ring familiar, having circulated widely on the internet. I've been pleased to see my thoughts appear on more than a million internet sites since 2009, and, today, one or another of my items is quoted on Twitter about every five minutes.

It is difficult to protect one's creative rights to short writings such as these. I am accustomed to seeing my items credited to others, often to the famous. This book, like my earlier one, *Round Up The Usual Subjects*, is a hopeful attempt to lay claim to some part of my work. That said, I do encourage the non-commercial use of my items, asking only attribution. I expect that commercial users will contact me for permission.

Robert Brault
bobbrault@att.net

# Thoughts

## Appendix

# Preface

As an introduction, let me repeat a part of the preface to my earlier book, *Round Up The Usual Subjects.*

*"In 1961, while in college, I sold a Picturesque Speech item to Reader's Digest. So began an avocation that has endured to this day. For the next thirty years, I programmed computers by day and wrote aphorisms by night. Some 1200 items made it into magazines and newspapers between 1961 and 1994.*

*"In 2009, seven years into retirement (and after a fifteen-year respite from writing), I launched an internet blog, called A Robert Brault Reader. My hope was to find a new audience for my published writings. To my surprise, the effort reawakened the old muse, and new thoughts began to flow.*

*"The blog was noticed by Terri Guillemets at The Quote Garden, the internet's most popular quote site. She soon was showcasing some 400 of my items, each with a hyperlink back to my site. Soon thereafter, a Google search would routinely turn up a million sites*

*quoting my items. Today, although I blog only occasionally, I find myself quoted on Twitter several hundred times each day."*

This new book, like the first, is primarily a selection of quotes from the blog, but I've added fresh quotes to almost every section and have interspersed throughout the book a variety of other writings. These consist of poems, recollections, short vignettes, humor pieces and an occasional op-ed style viewpoint. For the most part, these writings are taken from the blog, but I have not hesitated, here and there, to enhance them a bit.

I decided early on to intersperse the quotes and the other writings rather than present them in two separate sections. I found that most of the writings could be loosely associated with a quote topic; for example, my piece, "Why Not Flowers and Lace This Mother's Day?" seems an appropriate addition to my page of "Mom" quotes. The association is a bit loose at times, I confess, but I do like the idea of relieving the relentless procession of quotes with an occasional poem or essay.

The book, I should caution, is very much a miscellaneous collection. It alternates the serious and the silly, the thoughtful and the whimsical. And because it is organized as a quote book, alphabetically, these changes in mood come at you rather randomly. One section might draw a tear and the very next try to tickle your funny bone. Be prepared for something of a roller coaster ride.

As to the nature of the content, let me again quote the preface to my earlier book, *Round Up The Usual Subjects:*

*"The thoughts, for the most part, are geared to tried and true virtues -- to faith, hope and charity, to pluck and optimism, to tolerance , compassion and understanding. Mixed in, you will find a healthy dollop of the wry, the sly and the facetious, but you will find no malice.*

*Will you find wisdom in these pages? Yes, but only the wisdom you bring to them. My goal is to put into words that which we all know full well but seldom express. The deal, as I tell my blog readers, is that I supply the words, you supply the insight. "*

That said, I do hope you enjoy the book.

Robert Brault
June 2015

~~~

*Each day, awakening, are we asked to paint the sky blue? Need we coax the sun to rise or flowers to bloom? Need we teach birds to sing or children to laugh or lovers to kiss? No, though we think the world imperfect, it surrounds us each day with its perfections. We are not asked to create a perfect world; we are asked only to celebrate it.*

~~~

# Achievement

### Keynote Thought

*No matter what your goal, if you aren't happy
striving for it, you won't be happy achieving it.*

~~~

### Observations

*To achieve success, you can't let failure stop
you.  To achieve great success, you can't let
success stop you.*

~~~

*The great enemy of achievement is a schedule
already full.*

~~~

*It is hard sometimes, when nothing's stopping
you, to know what's stopping you.*

~~~

## Achievement

*Life is too short to wait for an answer,*
*especially when the answer is nearly always,*
*"It's up to you."*

~~~

*If your only goal is to achieve security, there are*
*two things you will never achieve: (1) security;*
*(2) anything else.*

~~~

*There is always a good excuse, always a reason*
*not to. The hardest freedom to win is the*
*freedom from our excuses.*

~~~

*More important sometimes than perseverance is*
*the knack of avoiding obstacles that are not in*
*your path.*

~~~

*No one pays us for our time and effort; we are*
*paid to produce something, and it's important to*
*constantly remind ourselves what it is.*

~~~

*You can waste a lot of time debating whether the only way is the easiest way.*

~~~

*What can be sadder than to realize that you had the key but never tried the lock.*

~~~

## If You Want My Advice

*Never let probability stop you. It is, and always has been, a notorious liar.*

~~~

*Be the dreamer who can rise to action.*
*Be the person of action who can pause to dream.*

~~~

# Adversity

### Keynote Thought

*So often when the obstacles in your path can't be overcome, it's not your path.*

~~~

### Observations

*Failure would be a bad thing if it didn't reopen so many opportunities.*

~~~

*The last time I failed, it made me double my effort, and it worked so well that I'm thinking of failing again.*

~~~

*The thing to realize, when everyone seems to doubt you, is that everyone has not been born yet.*

~~~

# Aging

### Keynote Thought

*Two things you discover as you get older --
you're not any wiser, and behind the wrinkles,
you're not any older, either.*

~~~

### Observations

*Who does not wish to be beautiful and clever
and rich and to have back, in old age, the time
spent trying to be any of them?*

~~~

*There is a time in life when you not only have
bittersweet memories, but you make bittersweet
plans.*

~~~

*The less time you have left, the more you like to
spend it with people who are glad to see you.*

~~~

*Eventually you realize that your whole life has been preparation, and you begin to wonder if the rest might be preparation, too.*

~~~

*You find in old age that it is possible to revisit the past, the one requirement being that you come as you are.*

~~~

A Reflection

*An old woman looks in a mirror, recalls a little girl with a rag doll, and wonders what became of the little girl.*

~~~

Could Be Verse

*The mind, as you age,*
*Is an artist, it seems.*
*Monet paints your mem'ries,*
*Picasso your dreams.*

~~~

## You Get To An Age...

*... when even your subconscious doesn't have any desires.*

*... when Sloth is the only one of the Seven Deadly Sins you still have energy for.*

~~~

## Speaking For Myself

*I just got back from a seance where everybody sat around resurrecting ghosts from the past. Wait, that was my class reunion.*

~~~

*I hear there's been a ghost sighting in my old hometown.  Funny, I was just back there the other day.*

## Dry, Sly and Wry

*You get to an age when the only way you meet new people is when you drive into their living room.*

~~~

# Apology

### Keynote Thought

*If I had it to do over, there'd be a hand I'd take
and a silence I'd break.*

~~~

### Observation

*We deny an apology to the person who deserves
it, and then one day they are gone, and we
apologize to anyone who will listen.*

~~~

*There is no due date on an apology.  If it is
owed, it is overdue.*

~~~

*If you are truly sorry you caused someone pain,
then God will not be the first of whom you ask
forgiveness.*

~~~

# Arts and Letters

### Keynote Thought

*Whatever the art form, it is about capturing a moment and storing it out of the reach of time.*

~~~

### Observations

*That portion of reality that can be composed within a frame can be understood.*

~~~

*The first goal of writing is to have one's words read successfully.*

~~~

*Ah, but a man's reach should exceed his grasp, said Browning, and so it has, extended by the length of pen and brush.*

~~~

# The Author Goes To Paris

## *Author's Note:*

In the fall of 2008, Joan and I made our first ever visit to Paris.   The focus of our visit was the Louvre, the Impressionist exhibits at the Musee d'Orsay and the home and gardens of Claude Monet in Giverny.  We stayed at a small hotel on the Left Bank and dined at restaurants and cafes in Saint Germain.  Following are a few impressions of that experience.

~~~

*To visit Paris is to relive a memory, a previous visit not required.*

~~~

## The Champs

There is an instant nostalgia you feel as a couple in Paris. The words from *Casablanca*, "We will always have Paris," seem to have been written for you alone. The feeling builds as you stroll up the Champs Elysees toward the Arc de Triomphe.

The avenue seems endless; the Arc looms in a blue haze, seeming always in the far distance. You move as if in slow-motion, the focus of some hidden camera, other strollers just figures in a blurred background.

*Paris seemed our private park*
*For us alone its charm beguiled*
*For us the Champs stretched to the Arc*
*For us the Mona Lisa smiled.*

~~~

## *The Louvre*

At the Louvre, the crowd gathers in a semicircle, roped off to a distance of about thirty feet from Da Vinci's masterpiece. People jostle to get to the front, so as to turn to a friend's camera and get a photo of themselves with the Mona Lisa in the background. If you stand off a bit and take in this scene, the Mona Lisa seems to look past the crowd, her eye catching yours, her enigmatic smile intended for you personally.

~~~

*I imagine the young Madonna Lisa del Giocondo posing for her famous portrait, and it occurs to her that in all her life to come, whenever she gazes into a looking glass, she will behold the Mona Lisa – and a strange little smile comes across her face.*

~~~

## *The Left Bank*

*And Satan said to the Lord, "I could make you
Hemingway in Paris in the 1920's." And the
Lord said, "Get away, Satan. For it is written
that you will not tempt the Lord thy God."*

~~~

We are seated at a sidewalk café in Saint
Germain, my bride with her café noir, I with my
schooner of Leffe beer. It is easy enough
to fancy that I am the young Hemingway in 1925,
at work on *The Sun Also Rises*. Perhaps, this day,
the writing has gone well, the sentences honest
and true. We sit happily. It is a good time
between us and we do not speak. It is good to sit
and listen to the noise of the street. The beer is
fresh and good and I finish it with pleasure. A
few raindrops patter on the café awning. We get
up and walk back to the hotel in the rain.

~~~

## The Monet Gardens

*The autumn glow of Giverny*
*Shown velvet soft on you and me,*
*No breeze astir, no gust to sway*
*The lily pond of Claude Monet.*

~~~

We stood at the foot of Monet's lily pond, looking across at the Japanese footbridge. I glanced from the actual scene to the Monet print in my hand. It seemed, as I compared the impression to the reality, that Mother Nature had not quite captured it. I realized then that I had long ago fashioned from Monet's impression my own imagined reality. And it had little to do with the lily pond at Giverny.

~~~

*The artist gazes upon a reality and creates his own impression. The viewer gazes upon the impression and creates his own reality.*

~~~

# Attitude

## Keynote Thought

*Nothing in life means anything unless someone cares, and the whole trick is to keep being that someone.*

~~~

## Observations

*You begin to find what you're looking for in life when you begin to look for what you're finding.*

~~~

*If you could trade lives with a happy person, he or she would be just as happy with yours.*

~~~

*I have no idea what heaven is like, but I know people who will enjoy it, and I know people who won't.*

~~~

# Be Yourself

## Keynote Thought

*Always be demanding of the person you are --
and forgiving of the person you were.*

*~~~*

## Observations

*A moment in life you never forget is the first
time you found the courage not to blame
yourself.*

*~~~*

*Of what use to get what you want in life if you
must become someone else to get it?*

*~~~*

*In the end you don't so much find yourself as
you find someone who knows who you are.*

*~~~*

## If You Want My Advice

*Present yourself always*
*As who you would be,*
*And that is the person*
*The world will see.*

~~~

*If you don't want to be thought of as just*
*another face in the crowd, stop answering to*
*that description.*

~~~

*Never be limited by what the world thinks you*
*are, because the world doesn't know, and*
*tomorrow it won't care."*

~~~

*There are always people who think they have*
*you all figured out.  Treasure them.  They are*
*your advantage in life.*

~~~

*If you let people treat you like a nobody, you*
*have nobody to blame.*

~~~

*Sometimes people get the wrong impression about us because that is the one we keep making.*

~~~

*Eventually people come to understand you, and you wonder why you ever thought that would improve things.*

~~~

### Dry, Sly And Wry

*There's nothing like an old photo of yourself to remind you how many different people have hid out behind that same face.*

~~~

*Ever wonder why people think you should know better when you've never given them any reason to think so?*

~~~

*There are secrets I will take to my grave -- and others I'll feel safer having cremated.*

~~~

*All your life you pretend to be someone else, and it turns out you were someone else pretending to be you.*

~~~

### Speaking For Myself

*I have been many different people in my life, no two of which, I think, would have been likely to exchange Christmas cards.*

~~~

*Yes, I worry that someone will discover the truth about me -- and not tell me what it is.*

~~~

*Truth is, I am still searching for myself -- and grateful to anyone who can tell me where I was last seen.*

~~~

*I am a private person, but I'll tell you this about myself -- if you start massaging my shoulders, don't expect me to tell you to stop.*

~~~

**Be Yourself**

*It's possible, I think, to become the person you were born to be and decide you can do better.*

~~~

*Perhaps if people really knew me they would understand me, but I'd rather be misunderstood than really known.*

~~~

*I've learned this about myself -- that beneath the superficial exterior breathes an inner spirit that just wants to party.*

~~~

*Yes, I worry about the craziest things, but better me than someone less qualified.*

~~~

# Belief

## Keynote Thought

*To believe only what you know to be true is to seriously under-appreciate the possibilities of belief.*

~~~

## Observations

*Anyone can believe on the evidence. It takes an inquisitive mind to believe on the strange, unaccountable lack of evidence.*

~~~

*The difference between what we suppose and what we believe is that we usually know why we suppose something.*

~~~

*Sometimes there are words you haven't heard in so long, you almost think you might believe them again.*

*Many people consult God, but few consult God for the purpose of hearing a different opinion.*

~~~

*There is no belief so preposterous that something more preposterous cannot be cited as further proof.*

~~~

*When we sacrifice truth to some self-serving belief, we tend to believe it tenaciously, for it has come at such great sacrifice.*

~~~

## Speaking For Myself

*You can hold beliefs that give you an advantage in life, but, please, don't go around calling them principles.*

~~~

*I like to give people the benefit of the doubt, since I am rarely certain, and certainty rarely benefits anyone anyway.*

~~~

# Childhood

## Keynote Thought

*We do not realize how fragile a thing childhood is until it becomes our turn to create it for our kids.*

~~~

## Observations

*The world knows how to straighten out a spoiled child but never makes it up to a child deprived.*

~~~

*Before you discourage a child, recall your own childhood, and consider what damage to your self-confidence you now believe was temporary.*

~~~

*It takes a while, but eventually you realize that the people who were always there for the special occasions of your childhood had other things to do.*

# Civility

## Keynote Thought

*We undervalue the courage of common civility,
for what do we know of another person's day, of
their worries and anxieties, of how deep into
their innermost resources they had to reach for
that gracious smile, that pleasant hello.*

~~~

## Observations

*How small a nod it would take, how fleeting a smile, to give someone you meet today a sense of self-worth.*

~~~

*If today you can't be anything else to anyone, you can be the passing stranger who nodded hello.*

~~~

*Sometimes civility is not just saying hello but dropping what you're doing to say hello.*

~~~

*It's a good day when everyone you meet thinks a little more of themselves for the encounter.*

~~~

*There is no effect more disproportionate to its cause than the pleasure bestowed by a small compliment.*

~~~

# The Woman In The Checkout Line

At the end, the Alzheimer's had left his mother a lost, old woman who would sit all day in her geriatric chair staring off into the distance. He would visit her at the church home and sit by her side, trying his best to lure the old light back into her eyes, hoping to see for just a moment the spark of recognition that would sometimes reappear out of the blue.

On their last day together she was particularly feeble, and the afternoon had been long with silence. He had turned sadly to leave when he felt her hand reach for his. When he looked back into her eyes, they were soft and alive, and he could see that his mother recognized him. He felt her hand tighten around his. She leaned close and said, in words just above a whisper, "There was a woman in the checkout line who thought you were the most beautiful baby."

That was all. Soon her eyes went dull, and there was no elaboration, and he knew that none would come. The next morning, the call came from the home, and they told him that his mother had died in the night.

In the years that followed he thought often about his mother's last words to him and about the woman in the checkout line. She was in his thoughts when he wrote, "Sometimes the most lasting memory is of the smallest kindness," and again, "There is no effect more disproportionate to its cause than the happiness bestowed by a small compliment."

There was a woman once who took a moment to compliment a young mother on her baby. Did she ever think again of her kind gesture? Did she imagine that her words would be carried in another person's memory for a lifetime? Did she guess that fifty years later, a dying old woman, searching her crippled memory for words to console a grieving son, would say to him, "There was a woman in the checkout line who thought you were the most beautiful baby."

~~~

# Commitment

*To commit to someone in life is to give up a thousand amusements for a single happiness.*

~~~

## <u>Observation</u>

*You have to decide what your duty is, or else others will tell you what it is -- and they will seem to know.*

~~~

*Of what use is freedom of choice if we always choose freedom and never choose choice?*

~~~

*Not everything we do each day is from love or a promise made, but that is the place to start.*

~~~

*You will be many different people in the course of your lifetime, so be a little careful of the promises you make for them.*

~~~

## How True, How True

*If you awoke one morning to find all your commitments met, what would you do? Right, you'd make six new commitments by sunset.*

~~~

## Speaking For Myself

I *do not awaken each day to an array of choices. I awaken to a clear duty born of the choices I have made. And to what have I sacrificed my freedom? To the life I wish to live and to the people I wish to live it with.*

~~~

# Compromise

### Keynote Thought

*Only among principled parties can there be compromise, and, of necessity, it must appear to be a compromise of principle. In fact, it is a discovery of principle, accomplished by leaving on the table prejudices and self-interests that only posed as principles. In the end, each party leaves the table more truly principled for the compromise.*

~~~

# Consolation

### Keynote Thought

*Sometimes a silent hug is the only thing to say.*

~~~

### Observation

*They seem so fumbling and foolish, the words of consolation we offer to another.  But then one day it becomes our turn to hear them, and how consoling to us those words become and how cherished the friend who stands there, fumbling for them.*

~~~

# Courage

### Keynote Thought

*There can be heroism in the moment, but courage is always in the day-to-day.*

~~~

### Observations

*It is an act of valor to coax someone down from a ledge, for nearly always we are reaching out from our own ledge.*

~~~

*They are also heroes who stand and cheer the parade -- and quietly return to their uncelebrated lives.*

~~~

*Sometimes courage is just a matter of having thought about what you would do if the situation ever came up.*

~~~

# The Daily Hassle

### Keynote Thought

*It's not just you.  No one gets out of bed in the morning and is entirely happy with the decision.*

~~~

### Observations

*It helps if you don't see it as traffic but as a thousand individuals resolved to push on another day.*

~~~

*There is a reason you were born -- and a bunch of things you've got to do today regardless.*

~~~

*Evening, and home I go, commuting from a world that doesn't listen to a world that has heard it a thousand times.*

~~~

*In everyday life, one thing leads to another, and usually just when you think it already has.*

~~~

*If you knew that some day you would live happily ever after, would you necessarily want to start today?*

~~~

*What you find in life's shell game is that it's hardest to follow the pea when you're the pea.*

~~~

*To survive, one must do what the situation calls for, and sometimes what it calls for is a cry for help.*

~~~

## How True, How True

*No matter what your complaint, there is a number to call where you will be told that you are the first person ever to complain about it.*

~~~

### Speaking For Myself

*Each morning I wake up with pretty much the same thought, "How can I get better results from waking up?"*

~~~

*Some mornings you wake up to the smell of the coffee, and some mornings you wake up to the smell of the halibut from last night's supper.*

~~~

### Dry, Sly and Wry

*There are days when you think, "Nobody's perfect, but does everybody have to prove it all at once?"*

~~~

### A Question

*Ever have a day when you can't get started on anything because nothing else can wait?*

~~~

## Billboards Seen Along The Daily Commute

"Three Miles to JERRY'S SMELL-THE-ROSES
DRIVE-THRU"

~~~

"CONTEMPLATIVE RELIGIOUS RETREATS -
Free Internet"

~~~

"Attention Working Mothers. Turn Your Spare
Time Into Cash! "

~~~

"Busy execs, Enjoy a Leisurely Vacation in Half
the Time!"

~~~

"ROAD LESS TRAVELED BY GETAWAYS.
Twice-a-day flights from all major hubs."

~~~

# Dancing

## Keynote Thought

*Dancing is moving to the music without stepping on anyone's toes, pretty much the same as life.*

~~~

## Observations

*Ballroom dancing is a meeting of the eyes, with various options for keeping the feet separate.*

~~~

*With due credit to Ginger Rogers, my wife can dance backwards, in heels, and while talking on a cellphone.*

~~~

*As for my own dancing, I occasionally trip the light fantastic, but she always gets back on her feet.*

~~~

# Destiny

### Keynote Thought

*On a windswept hill*
*By a billowing sea,*
*My destiny sits*
*And waits for me.*

~~~

### Observations

*Life starts out as partly destiny and partly free*
*will, but then you have kids and it's all destiny.*

~~~

*Chance has this in common with destiny -- that*
*it's just as apt to be chiseled in stone.*

~~~

*It is curious that people who profess no belief in*
*destiny still complain of their lot in life.*

~~~

*Sometimes Fate brings two people together by causing one to misinterpret a smile.*

~~~

*It remains an open question -- are we marionettes or are we creatures of free will who just happen to have a lot of jerky reflexes?*

~~~

<u>Dry, Sly and Wry</u>

*Life holds true to destiny about as much as the movie holds true to the book.*

~~~

# Driving

### Road Sign

*"ROAD WORK NEXT TEN MILES" means that you are approaching a median area where construction equipment is parked so that fines may be doubled.*

~~~

### Observations

*An important driving aid at my age is someone in the passenger's seat shouting "Dear God!"*

~~~

*One advantage of failing eyesight is that you think other drivers are giving you the thumbs up.*

~~~

*The most common decision made at the eleventh hour is that we'd better start looking for a motel.*

# Faith

## Keynote Thought

*Things happen in life that make us question our faith when perhaps they ought to make us question our life.*

~~~

## Observations

*They are Godseekers both, the churchgoing believer and the pilgrim to an unknown shrine.*

~~~

*It is easier to come to faith from doubt than to return to faith from certainty.*

~~~

*If you give it a central place in your life, what does it matter if you call it faith or you call it doubt?*

~~~

# Family

## Keynote Thought

*A family is a group of people who keep mistaking you for someone you were as a kid.*

*~~~*

## Observations

*Every family has arguments that scare the dog. The concern is when they alarm the cat.*

*~~~*

*A common fallacy in large families is that the last person to use it knows where it is.*

*~~~*

*In a household of toddlers and pets, you discover this rule of thumb about happy families -- they are two-thirds incontinent.*

*~~~*

## Speaking For Myself

*I have never complained of my loved ones taking me for granted, because that was my goal from the start.*

~~~

*I guess I define "immediate family" as the people who, when you need help, show up immediately.*

~~~

*Whatever happens to someone I love happens to me, which can make for a full day, let me tell you.*

~~~

## Dry, Sly and Wry

*Somewhere in everyone's family tree are two people who shouldn't have got married and shouldn't have had kids.*

~~~

# Friendship

### Keynote Thought

*May you have a good friend to keep you out of trouble -- and a best friend to help you go looking for it.*

~~~

### Observations

*How often the answer to our prayers is to become the answer to someone else's prayers.*

~~~

*As a friend you first give your understanding, then you try to understand.*

~~~

*What do we ask of friendship except to be taken for who we pretend to be -- and without having to pretend.*

~~~

*There are times in a friendship when one must
be friend enough for both.*

~~~

*A best friend is someone who knows your
virtues but thinks your failings more than make
up for them.*

~~~

*Making friends is the art of seeing something to
like in a person and stopping right there.*

~~~

*You can break up a marriage and still be
friends, but it's harder to do with a friendship.*

~~~

*Some people need a cross to bear, and there are
times as a friend when you need to be that cross.*

~~~

*It's a good friend who, when you want the truth,
knows what truth you want.*

~~~

# God

## Keynote Thought

*There is this about a self-evident truth -- that it can never be proved, because any proof offered will be less self-evident than the premise. All attempts to prove it will appear to fail, and in failing, they will cast doubt upon the premise. Such is the case with the existence of God. It is a self-evident truth obscured by dubious proofs.*

~~~

## Observations

*Science can reconstruct Tyrannosaurus Rex
from a fossilized bone and a fancied footprint
but cannot reconstruct God from the whole of
Creation.*

~~~

*You wonder -- if the CSI team were to examine
the evidence of Creation, would they conclude
that the crime committed itself?*

~~~

*To the believer, Creation is God's handiwork.
To the scientist, it is just something that
happened in the normal course of miracles.*

~~~

## Speaking For Myself

*I feel more kinship with folks who pray each
day for divine guidance than with those
equipped at birth with a divine guidance
system.*

~~~

# Government

### Keynote Thought

*A nation flourishes sharing the same belief system and disintegrates sharing the same denial system.*

~~~

### Observations

*Thinking that a new government is the answer is like thinking that the road would be safer if there were a new troll under the bridge.*

~~~

*Every republic must periodically put down rebels determined to restore its constitution.*

~~~

*You wonder why it's always the solution and never the problem that gets mired in government red tape.*

~~~

## <u>Dry, Sly and Wry</u>

*There are statistics the government couldn't release at all if it weren't for recent advances in lying.*

~~~

*Seems like no one wants to eliminate a government program until you've been paying into it all your life.*

~~~

*For every question you have about a government program, there's an agency that isn't the right place to inquire about it.*

~~~

*One thing you need never fear in a democracy is ignorance without representation.*

~~~

*How will the U.S. pay off its debt to China? It will rob Peter to pay Cheng.*

~~~

# Happiness

### Keynote Thought

*Once I saw happiness as a destination and sought a shortcut.  Now I see happiness as a road and treasure its every bend.*

~~~

## Observations

*No matter how carefully you plan your life,
your happiness will come down to someone who
one day just walked into it.*

~~~

*It is a sad thing when everything in life that
might make you happy is ever so slightly
outside your comfort zone.*

~~~

*Sometimes, crazy as it seems, happiness can be
found among those who wish it for us.*

~~~

*I think if we ever succeeded in simplifying our
lives, we'd discover that most of our happiness
was in the complications.*

~~~

*You can look ahead to happiness, and you can
look backward on it, but it's so hard to notice it
to your left or right.*

~~~

*If you are not on your guard, putting on your unhappiness in the morning can become as instinctive as putting on your clothes.*

~~~

*You can't make someone happy by making yourself miserable, no matter how diligently you keep up your end of the bargain.*

~~~

*So often the shortest distance to happiness is the length of an about-face.*

~~~

*Sometimes you wish for an easy life, but fate intervenes and makes it a happy one.*

~~~

*It is easier to find  happiness than to look no further.*

~~~

*You can be sad recalling sad times, but if you really want to be sad, recall happy times.*

~~~

*One measure of a happy life is how many things you get a high from that don't have any street value.*

~~~

*You seldom find happiness by increasing the number of things you own that have nothing to do with it.*

~~~

*Do not ask, "What reason do I have to be happy?" Instead ask, "To what purpose can I attach my happiness?"*

~~~

*To be happy, you must fancy that everything you have is a gift, and you the chosen, though you worked your tail off for every bit of it.*

~~~

*There is no more engaging quality in a human being than the ability to be made happy.*

~~~

# The Holidays

### Keynote Thought

*What would holiday shopping be without strangers -- without people jostling all about you?  And how miraculous that each year they suddenly, magically appear.  You go out to the mall, and there they are, in all shapes and sizes, young and old, tall and short, populating your holiday season just as surely as if they had answered a call from central casting.*

~~~

# A Holiday Cocktail Party Is Where --

*-- every year you have the same conversation with the same couple about who you both still are.*

*-- some stranger learns more about you in an hour than your spouse has learned in a lifetime.*

*-- the host and hostess attempt to bring compatible people together by separating married couples.*

*-- there is a rotation that brings married couples back together again every twenty minutes.*

*-- you are always sorry you wrote anything on a napkin.*

*-- nobody thinks it's late until the first couple leaves and then everybody thinks it's late.*

~~~

## Speaking For Myself

*The thing about going to a holiday cocktail party is that it forces you to grapple with the question, "Who am I?"-- because somebody's bound to ask.*

~~~

*There are couples who will always be first to arrive at a party no matter how many times they drive around the block.*

~~~

*But I love a cocktail party.  It's the only place where you can meet people who share your desperate desire to be somewhere else.*

~~~

## If You Want My Advice

*Never swear to lose five pounds over the holidays unless you have already lost the first ten.*

~~~

# New Year's Eve With Some New Acquaintances

For many years, my wife and I have saved an empty champagne bottle from each New Year's Eve celebration.

These old Korbels and Andres and Taylors sit dust-covered in a corner of our basement. Occasionally, when I'm in the mood to reminisce, I'll go downstairs and wipe the dust from the labels.

"Byron Drive, 1998" – the place and year are always in my handwriting. I'm the one who gets the ball rolling each year, the one who starts the empty bottle around so that everyone can sign it.

Scattered over the label are the scrawled names: "Curt...Nancy...Don...Sybil." These are the friends and acquaintances who shared our celebration that New Year's Eve.

The signing of champagne bottles started as a whim, but we kept it up over the years. I'm glad we did. There's a story in these old bottles that is not told in any of our family photo albums. They capture a thread in our lives that might otherwise be lost.

The memories they hold are not, for the most part, of family or even long-time friends. Fittingly, they are memories of old acquaintances.

In most years, the labels tell us, we have spent New Year's Eve with people we've known only a short while. We've raised a glass with new neighbors, colleagues on new jobs, members of community and social groups we've just joined.

Only a few of these relationships have survived the years. The names on the labels keep changing.

It's curious how the milestones of our lives can be tracked in the changing names on these bottle labels: new jobs, new neighborhoods, new interests and commitments. They're like the logbook of a journey. And they're a reminder of something that lately we've forgotten – that there's a valued part of our lives that has always been measured in acquaintanceship.

In recent years, there have been fewer names on the labels, and they are often the same names. We've taken to spending New Year's Eve with a few close friends. We've settled down, become less active; we're not into acquaintanceship these days.

If these recent labels are a logbook, it appears

they are logging a journey's end. This bothers me. When I compare these recent labels to earlier ones that are covered with so many names, I feel a sense of loss.

It saddens me to think of those old acquaintanceships that we carelessly let go. And it saddens me to realize that we have let a part of our life's journey shrink away – the part that was charted in our new acquaintanceships.

Recently we joined a new group for the first time in years. We're going to celebrate New Year' s Eve with acquaintances this year. We've invited our friends to join us. There should be room on the champagne bottle for everyone's name – if we all write small.

~~~

# Hometown

### Keynote Thought

*You don't realize how inaccurate network TV reporting is until they do a story in your hometown.*

~~~

### Speaking For Myself

*How lazy is my hometown?  It is so lazy that the stopped clock on the church steeple is right only once a day.*

~~~

*And the town fathers are debating whether to do a twice-a-week pickup on the 911 post office box.*

~~~

*And small?  My hometown is so small that it doesn't have a town drunk.  They have to share a regional drunk with two other towns.*

~~~

## Notes From Back Home

The recession has hit home. Over at Mort's Diner, they say that not only is business down but folks are finishing up their cole slaw.

Otherwise, all's normal. Aunt Cora's been making the rounds of the summer tag sales, stocking up on items for her fall tag sale.

Grandma's just back from her class reunion, where she says everyone got teary-eyed over the photos from their last class reunion.

Grandpa's been recalling his school days. Says he never got an 'A' in Self-Esteem. Back then it was a 'D' in Conduct.

Over at Alf's Used Car Mecca they're advertising a five-star beauty they say was last owned by a doctor who used it only on house calls.

Meanwhile, Junior came home from school all glum-faced to say, "I lost the spelling cee."

Cousin Ben reports that wife Maebelle's crash diet is advancing steadily through the planning stages.

The regulars over at the general store pooled wits and came up with an idea. Name the season's first hurricane Zelda and fool Mother Nature into calling it a year.

Aunt Josephine says Uncle Hank's computer learnin' is almost to the stage where he can point and click without moving his lips.

Zack Wormsley reports that his 1:00 PM flight out of County Airport took off at 3:45, listed ON TIME. Said Zack, "I guess they reckon one is a quarter of four."

Pa's been surveying Mr. Cole's new lawn next door and says there's always the chance ours will turn green with envy.

Banker Milhouse admits that the local economy is depressed but urges everyone to be calm since it's an absolute prerequisite to remaining calm.

Meanwhile, Aunt Cora observes that it's getting harder and harder to worry needlessly.

Over at the Hatfield's, Morris reports that Gert is still putting off being happy until such time as she can be happier.

Pastor Ballou was reckoning the other day that for every sinner around here, there are three repenters.

Cousin Arabelle says she knows she's being punished for her sins. She just wonders when she gets to commit them.

Aunt Georgie writes from the city that's she's divorced again. Last time it was lipstick on the collar; this time it's lip prints on the mirror.

Grandpa's just back from town hall where he says just once he'd like to complain to someone who didn't need him to calm down first.

Pa's been advising the neighbor's boy on a profession, observing that a plumber never looked up a bond trader in the yellow pages.

Uncle Hank says he doesn't reckon his dog has human feelings, but he sure lets you know when you hurt his instincts.

Cousin Morris opines that if the Lord wanted him to see the sunrise, He would have scheduled it later in the day.

Ma is just back from old man Grimshaw's funeral where she said friends fondly recalled the things he used to complain about the least.

And Ma baked up a rhubarb pie and took it over to Mr. Cobb, the widower down the street. "It was a kindness I've been putting off," she said, "and didn't seem like putting it off was making it any kinder."

~~~

# Hope

## Keynote Thought

*What you must realize about a hopeless situation is that it's just a situation -- you are supplying the hopelessness.*

~~~

## Observations

*Hope is not a plan, unless hope is all you have left,  then it's a plan.*

*~~~*

*Despair is nearly always a still shot taken from a movie that is not over.*

*~~~*

*It is so sad, and so avoidable, to awaken one morning to realize that you are no longer anyone's hope.*

*~~~*

*Why chase a hopeless dream?  I dunno, maybe for the dream, maybe for the chase, maybe to meet another hopeless dreamer.*

*~~~*

*There is always sufficient reason for despair, but there is never sufficient purpose.*

*~~~*

*They say it's never too late, but sometimes it is,
and you have to wait a day or two before it isn't
again.*

~~~

*Few are hopeless who can look ahead in this life,
and no one is hopeless who can look beyond it.*

~~~

*A shattered dream is like broken glass.  You
never quite sweep up all the pieces.*

~~~

*The lesson of Good Friday is to never give up
hope -- or at least give it another 48 hours.*

~~~

## Speaking For Myself

*There are spring days when my winter despair
seems an offense against the Creator and my
black mood an affront to the blue sky.*

~~~

# Humankind

### Keynote Thought

*Perhaps God will pity a race that sought its better angels but found only its lesser demons.*

~~~

### Observations

*We accept the weakness in others that makes them just like us, but we despise the weakness in ourselves that makes us just like them.*

~~~

*People are defined by the hardships they have faced or the hardships they have been spared -- and you can always tell which.*

~~~

*To know the innermost fears of anyone is to know the innermost fears of everyone.*

~~~

*No human being is anyone else's reward or punishment for anything.*

~~~

*The average person usually does the right thing, a reason perhaps why so many prefer to stay average.*

~~~

*Nothing brings people together like having the same deck stacked against them.*

~~~

*Evidence suggests that every life form on Earth was given the choice of intelligence or perfection, and all but one chose perfection.*

~~~

*It is a lonely circus that has but one clown.*

~~~

*I am a guest in your life.  You are a guest in mine.  Not something calling for a dress code maybe, but a little etiquette?*

~~~

*It's a tricky word -- "everybody." When you hear, "Everybody's doing it," it never includes you, and when you think, "Everybody knows that," it never includes anybody else.*

~~~

*What would happen if some fine morning you said, "Okay, today everyone I know gets a fresh start."*

~~~

*People judge us by first impression -- the better our first impression of them, the better they judge us.*

~~~

## Speaking For Myself

*I don't know if we're all God's children, but I know if I am, you are.*

~~~

*On the one hand, I would like to expect the best of every human being I meet. On the other hand, that would make me a dog.*

~~~

*Life is a series of events so arranged that if you don't know what someone else is going through, you will soon enough.*

~~~

*I've learned this -- that it is impossible to understand any human being using just what you know about them.*

~~~

### Dry, Sly and Wry

*On the Sixth Day, God created man, the sort of result you get when you go in to work on a Saturday.*

~~~

### A Brief History of Humankind

*Once there was an animal who was sent to fetch but could never figure out who sent him or what for.*

~~~

# Humble Pie

### Keynote Thought

*If you could eavesdrop on everything said about you, you'd spend most of your time waiting for the subject to come up.*

~~~

### Speaking For Myself

*I guess the reason I've never sought fame is the feedback I get from people who have already heard of me.*

~~~

*Given my demonstrated ability to do several fool things at once, I consider it progress to do one fool thing after another.*

~~~

*Having experienced both, I prefer being ignored to getting no attention at all.*

*As part of my latest diet regimen, I've given up banquets in my honor, which so far I'm sticking to pretty well.*

~~~

*Whenever somebody says, "I am humbled by this award," I wonder just how humbled they would be by never getting one.*

~~~

*The only award I ever won was from my golf club -- "Most Congenial Partner"  On accepting, I said, "I'm not only humbled by this award, I'm humiliated by it."*

~~~

## A Question

*If man is on top of the food chain, where exactly is the mosquito?*

~~~

# The Interview

### Keynote Thought

*As a job applicant, there are two things you must ask of your interviewer. You must ask for a precise description of the result wanted from the job, not the skill set required but the tangible deliverable desired. Then you must ask for the interviewer's attention as you describe the path to that result that begins in the chair you're sitting in, showing how along that path you, yourself, will determine the skills required and secure them as needed.*

~~~

# How To Ace Your Judgment Day Interview

*1. Be on time.*

*2. Dress conservatively (white robe, sandals, etc.)*

*3. Be alert, make direct eye contact.*

*4. Tell the Lord you've heard a lot about heaven and like what you hear.*

*5. When the Lord speaks, lean forward, look interested.*

*6. Be familiar with the Lord's background. ("I really liked your Ten Commandments.")*

*7. Be clear on where you want to be in five years.*

*8. Be honest about personal flaws. ("I tend to be too forgiving.")*

*9. Do not hesitate to underscore qualifications. ("I go to church every Easter.")*

*10. Make it clear that you'll accept the standard benefits package.*

~~~

# Justice

*Justice is justice.  It does not become mercy because you are forced to beg for it.*

~~~

## Observations

*The battle now and always is to ensure that justice remains admissible in a court of law.*

~~~

*Whatever justice is, it is not something decided by a 5-4 vote of the U.S. Supreme Court.*

~~~

*Better to serve a just God and discover He is forgiving than to serve a forgiving God and discover He is just.*

~~~

**Justice**

*You wonder what the world would be like if justice were not so often confused with revenge.*

~~~

## If You Want My Advice

*Never say that someone does not deserve mercy. Mercy is never deserved. If it were, it would be justice.*

~~~

*I've learned this about judging people -- you can have all the facts and not know the whole story.*

~~~

# Kids

## Keynote Thought

*Kids grow up whether you raise them or not, generally spending a lot more time growing up than being raised.*

~~~

## Observations

*While kids do not instruct their parents, they educate them wonderfully.*

~~~

*There is an entire branch of psychology specializing in children who will not join the common madness.*

~~~

*A question to ask, as parent or teacher, is whether a child who never won your approval ever knew it was available.*

~~~

**Kids**

What is a child's mind but a small world, and what is a teacher's job but to shine on it like the sun?

~~~

You can teach your kids to know better, but you can't teach them not to do it anyway.

~~~

When kids feel they have earned our respect, the last thing they want is our unconditional love.

~~~

Yes, it's a tired old world, but a kid can still find six fascinating detours from the school bus to the front door.

~~~

Never say anything to a child that you wouldn't want repeated in a child's words.

~~~

The tragedy of a sad child is that a child has such a capacity to be cheered up.

~~~

# Learning

## Keynote Thought

*There are things you learn the hard way, and things you just have to learn again.*

~~~

## Observations

*One is more apt to become wise by doing fool things than by reading wise sayings.*

~~~

*There are several ways to become an expert, self-appointment being the most common.*

~~~

*The trouble with thinking you're 100% right is that it's the only way you can be 100% wrong.*

~~~

## Learning

*Every day learn something new, and just as important, relearn something old.*

~~~

*One of life's ongoing mysteries is how one goes about becoming more ignorant.*

~~~

*It's a mistake, when life hands you a hard lesson, to think you can get back at life by not learning it.*

~~~

*Man will have replicated his own intelligence not when he teaches a computer to reason but when he teaches a computer to have a nagging feeling in its circuits.*

~~~

*The first requirement of learning is to have absolutely no idea what you want to hear.*

~~~

*It is a shame to trade your curiosity for a bunch of answers that make you wonder why you were ever curious.*

## Speaking For Myself

*I'll tell you what's scary -- it's scary to meet someone far more knowledgeable than you are who doesn't know a thing.*

~~~

*There are subjects in which I wish to become knowledgeable and subjects in which I wish to remain wise.*

~~~

*There are truths of which I have an inkling, but of most I have only a penciling.*

~~~

*At 21, I made age-21 mistakes. At 75, I'm making age-75 mistakes. But I learned to be 22, and I'm hoping to learn to be 76.*

~~~

# Life

### Keynote Thought

*We complain that life is not easy, but did we pray for an easy life or did we pray for happiness and fulfillment -- and did we suppose it would be easy?*

~~~

## Observations

*May it be said of you that you relished the dance of life and went out applauding the band.*

~~~

*Occasionally ask, "What is the connection between what I want most in life and anything I plan to do today?"*

~~~

*People aren't ignoring you. They are busy with their lives, and the way to stop feeling ignored is to get busy with yours.*

~~~

*If you never pause to look about you, it is possible to live a dull gray life under a blue sky.*

~~~

*Sometimes you must take the single step that starts the journey to discover that it is a journey of a single step.*

~~~

*What you discover about a dream come true is that you must keep dreaming it to make it stay true.*

~~~

*Maybe you never catch the dream you chase all your life, but it usually takes you up the road you want to travel.*

~~~

*In childhood we yearn to be grown-ups.  In old age we yearn to be kids.  It just seems that all would be wonderful if we didn't have to celebrate our birthdays in chronological order.*

~~~

## If You Want My Advice

*Always keep a list of priorities, but occasionally start from the bottom.*

~~~

*Get involved.  You don't want to reach the end of your life and discover that you successfully managed to stay out of it.*

~~~

*Do things while you can and while they still matter to you, because neither is a permanent state of affairs.*

~~~

*No matter how carefully you cover your tracks, you always  leave behind clues that place you at the scene of your life.*

~~~

<u>Speaking For Myself</u>

*A tiny complaint I have about life is that so many of its wake-up calls require you to die first.*

~~~

*What do I ask of life except to live yesterday over again and tomorrow in advance?*

~~~

*I have long suspected that life is a distraction, but probably not from anything important.*

~~~

### Ask Yourself This

*If you could apply for a life of ease, what exactly would you state as the purpose of your request?*

~~~

*Will you spend your life pushing a boulder uphill so that once uphill you will have a boulder to sit on while lamenting your life?*

~~~

### How True, How True

*Ever get the feeling that sometime early in your life there was a briefing you missed?*

~~~

### Once Heard

*"They were happy times, those days of struggle. I know it now, and what I will always thank God for, I knew it then."*

~~~

### *Life Is...*

*Life is  a set of reactions that aren't what you intend -- to a set of situations that aren't what they seem.*

~~~

*Life is a collection of moments that you might have appreciated more if you had only known they were moments.*

~~~

*Life is a series of family photos in which you keep moving to the rear until finally you're a portrait in the background.*

~~~

*Life is a quest for a fondly-imagined leisure which, when achieved, is spent fondly remembering the quest.*

~~~

*Life is many things, but above all others, it is the chance you've been waiting for.*

~~~

# Listening

## Keynote Thought

*It's amazing the ideas that pop into your head while people are saying them into your ear.*

*~~~*

## Observations

*If you look like somebody who's willing to listen, you hear a lot of explanations owed to other people.*

*~~~*

*There's a limit to how much information you can absorb while thinking of what you're going to say next.*

*~~~*

*You never have a person's fuller attention than when you're listening to them.*

*~~~*

# Logic

## Keynote Thought

*Logic is a method of reasoning that causes you to say at least six times a day, "This can't be happening!"*

~~~

## Observations

*The logic of many people amounts to this -- if A is true because B is true, and B is proved false, then praise God that A is still true.*

~~~

*I believe in cause and effect, although not necessarily in that order.*

~~~

*There are things happening today that don't make sense, and you dread the sense they would make if they did.*

~~

# Loss of a Child

*<u>Author's Note</u>:*

In 1995, after the Oklahoma City bombing, and again in 2013 , after the Newtown tragedy, I wrote several poems and brief thoughts for publication, two of which I share here.

I know that words are of little consolation  in the wake of losing a child, but time goes by and eventually we try to work through to an intellectual accommodation.  Words can have a place in the process.

I confess I'm a bit of an intruder in this realm, having never lost a child of my own. My poem, "Jessie's Piece,"  although written in the first person, does not reflect a personal experience but rather an outlook on life that I find appealing.  I hope no one takes exception to my sharing it.

~~~

# When, Lo, A Tiny Hand Takes Mine

*If there be consolation, it must come from knowing that others have suffered such grievous loss and have recovered to find purpose in their lives. We exist in a cycle of relentless restoration and renewal, a cycle in which the spring returns and that which seemed forever gone is reborn. Those who go before us lead the way, and who knows what divine purpose resides in a child taken from us prematurely.*

*Child lost, sometimes in dreams*
*I wander in an endless night,*
*When, lo, a tiny hand takes mine,*
*And leads me to the morning light.*

~~~

## Jessie's Piece

*The world's a jigsaw, once I thought,*
*With each of us a piece to fit,*
*A pre-determined grand design*
*And each of us a part of it.*

*I thought that God must surely have*
*A blueprint of His final goal,*
*And all who come into this life*
*Are meant to play some fated role.*

*But when my little Jessie died,*
*It seemed to me but sheer caprice.*
*Where fits a child in God's design*
*Who never lived to add her piece?*

*How often did I walk alone*
*To still the anguish in my heart,*
*To ask why God would make a plan*
*In which my child had no part.*

*One day, upon a village square,*
*I happened by a tiny shop.*
*What random step had led me there?*
*What in the window made me stop?*

*It was a quilt, a crazy quilt,*
*Each piece a brightly-colored patch,*
*A joyful, glowing work of art*
*From scraps you'd think would never match.*

*I looked upon the quilt in awe*
*To think a thing so oddly fine*
*Was stitched from fragments never made*
*To fit to anyone's design.*

*I wondered then if God might wish*
*That in this way His world be built,*
*Each life a motley-colored scrap*
*And He the weaver of the quilt.*

*If such be true, I realize,*
*My child's life, though short it be,*
*Is yet a joyful, shining patch*
*In God's eternal tapestry.*

*I looked upon the quilt and saw*
*A patch that seemed but sheer caprice,*
*So whimsical it made me smile.*
*I knew it was my Jessie's piece.*

~~~

# Love

*Love demands, friendship asks.*
*Love drains, friendship refreshes.*
*Love is jealous, friendship is broadminded.*
*Love constrains, friendship frees.*
*Love wants more, friendship takes what it gets.*

*Love sits by your bedside through the long night of illness.*
*Friendship pops in for a visit.*

~~~

## A Wish

*May you have the respect you earn, the gratitude you deserve, and the love that leaves you forever wondering how you could have been so lucky.*

~~~

## Observations

*In life you start out not knowing anything and end up knowing better. In love you start out knowing better and end up not knowing anything.*

~~~

*Love is at first a set of romantic fancies, which, as the years go by, you discard like training wheels, and you learn to love truly.*

~~~

*Is it so much that love asks -- that one day you be its strength and the next day its babe-in-arms?*

~~~

**Love**

*What we seek in the end is not unconditional love but a love for which we, uniquely in all the world, meet all the conditions.*

*~~~*

*To fall in love is not to enter the world of our dreams but to find someone who will take us by the hand and lead us out of it.*

*~~~*

*So often two people who see the same things as fun see the same thing as love.*

*~~~*

*There are people who can't say "I love you." They can only say, "I miss you."*

*~~~*

*It's a bit too late, after you've said, "I love you," to start parsing out the promises not included.*

*~~~*

*It's generally a good idea not to say "I love you" if there's something you don't mean by it.*

*~~~*

*Love may be blind, but like most who are blind, it knows pretty much where everything is.*

~~~

*It isn't sad enough when love dies. We must torture ourselves with the thought that it never was.*

~~~

*So often our loved ones mistake our understanding for approval, having already mistaken our love for understanding.*

~~~

*It seems that "love" ought to rhyme with "approve," but it doesn't, and at times you just have to live with it.*

~~~

*Sometimes love needs a rest from caring and so endures for an intolerable few hours the guilt of not caring.*

~~~

*You can as easily stop caring as you can go back and not start.*

**Love**

*There is a language of love, which is to say, a truth that does not tell all and a lie that does not deceive.*

~~~

*One never wishes so much to be hated as when love becomes indifference.*

~~~

*The heart has its reasons, and they aren't debate topics.*

~~~

<u>Speaking For Myself</u>

*I don't hate anyone.  The only people I know well enough to hate, I love*

~~~

# Marriage

### Keynote Thought

*Marriage is a multiplication of whatever you bring to it.*

~~~

### Observations

*Marriage has this in common with riding a Brahma bull -- it is judged less by style points than duration.*

~~~

*There is a private part of us we share with no one, and it is to this part of us that the marriage vows are addressed.*

~~~

*To be true to one another is not merely a promise; there are times in a marriage when it's your only plan.*

~~~

*Most marriages can survive better or worse.*
*The tester is all those years of exactly the same.*

~~~

*So often the person for whom you would climb*
*any mountain and swim any sea would settle*
*for a little conversation at dinner.*

~~~

## If You Want My Advice

*Never marry anyone that you can't picture*
*helping you go to the bathroom.*

~~~

## Whatever Works

*On their golden wedding anniversary, a couple*
*was asked to account for their long and happy*
*marriage. The husband said, "I try never to be*
*selfish. After all, there is no 'I' in the word*
*marriage."*

*The wife said, "For my part, I never correct my*
*husband's spelling."*

~~~

## <u>Dry, Sly and Wry</u>

*Statistics are unclear as to how many marriages have been saved by memories of a lavish wedding.*

~~~

*The basic flaw in marriage is that you can't marry an impartial third party.*

~~~

*Marriage between a man and woman is society's way of making sure that a woman gets a little mothering experience before she has her first child.*

~~~

## <u>Bed Fellows</u>

*If you snore on your back, you probably bear jab marks from someone who mistakenly thought you wouldn't snore on your side.*

~~~

# Meaning of Life

<u>Keynote Thought</u>

*To know the meaning of life, we must know the mind of God.  To find meaning in our own lives we must know only our own talents and abilities and recognize the opportunity that exists all around us to apply these gifts in the relief of human need.*

~~~

## Observations

*I think that God had thus instructed His answering service: "When they pray for understanding, give them hope."*

~~~

*Invariably our days get taken up with family responsibilities, our search for life's purpose sidetracked by finding it.*

~~~

*There exists in the human soul a sense of unworthiness, which if not an awareness of a divine purpose in life is pretty difficult to explain.*

~~~

*We are all waiting for answers. Life is pretty much what we do in the meantime.*

~~~

*Seems like you never hear that anything is part of a larger plan without wishing there were a smaller plan.*

~~~

## Perspective, Anyone?

*When compiling his great dictionary, the young Noah Webster travels to the Himalayas, where he climbs to the cave of the world's wisest man. "O, great sage," he says, "tell me the meaning of life."*

*The sage sits Noah at his feet and, with great solemnity, unfolds to him the meaning of life. When finished, he places a hand on the young man's shoulder and says, "Do you have any other questions, my son?"*

*Noah flips a page in his notebook and says, "You wouldn't know the meaning of lift, would you?"*

~~~

*One day the world will end , and everything human beings have ever done will fade into oblivion, and the one consolation will be that it probably has happened before.*

~~~

# Mind Games

### Keynote Thought

*Stored away in some brain cell is the image of a long-departed aunt you haven't thought of in 30 years. Stored away in another cell is the image of a pink pony stitched on your first set of baby pajamas. All it takes to get that aunt mounted on the back of that pony is to eat a slab of meatloaf immediately before going to bed.*

*~~~*

*I've concluded after many years that my mind works by process of elimination. Problem is, it hasn't eliminated anything yet.*

*~~~*

*So many things go through my mind that I never say. So many things that I say never go through my mind.*

*~~~*

# Miracles

*You can hope for a miracle in your life, or you can see your life as the miracle.*

~~~

## Observations

*There are times when you don't need a miracle, but you definitely need something unknown to science.*

~~~

*When a miracle happens, it is usually in the near proximity of someone who believed it would.*

~~~

*If you don't believe in miracles, it's wise to marry someone who does.*

~~~

*The believer prays for God's help.  It is the non-believer who must pray for a miracle.*

~~~

## Could Be The Answer

*Pastor to church member:  "You say that you don't believe in prayer and you don't believe in miracles?"*

*Member:  "That is true, pastor."*

*Pastor:  "Then, child, we'd better pray for a miracle."*

~~~

# Mom

### Keynote Thought

*What is a mom but the sunshine of our days and the north star of our nights.*

*~~~*

### Observations

*Mom is the one relative you can appeal to who will never look upon it as an appeal to your relationship.*

*~~~*

*A mom's hopes always exceed her expectations, and her encouragement always exceeds her hopes.*

*~~~*

*A mom knows all our hiding places, beginning with the very first.*

*~~~*

# Why Not Flowers And Lace This Mother's Day?

You know the scene. You've been twenty minutes at the card rack trying to find a Mother's Day number for Mom. It's no sale. Everything's too saccharine, too precious, too cutesy. The folks around you are in the same pickle. Every card on the rack has been handled twenty times. The stranger next to you says, "I'll give to your mother if you'll give to my mother." You think about it seriously.

But wait, not every card's been handled, not really, not those flowers-and-lace jobbies at the top of the rack. You know the ones I mean, the oversized ones in verse that begin, "What is a Mother?" – by Shirley Canby Stickie or Ida Soonbee Fulsome.

Too sentimental, everyone figures.

That's the thing about Mother's Day sentiments: they get sentimental if you don't watch out. Gratitude, appreciation, filial affection – they're easy to overdo, especially in verse. The ideal card, you figure, comes at them from an angle, by way of a catchy phrase, a subtle hint, a casual word or two.

Who doesn't recall the familiar movie scene where the hard-boiled coach says to the winning athlete, "Not bad, kid." Think of all that's implied in that simple expression: the bear hugs, the slaps on the back, the inexpressible pride. It's all there in those three understated words, "Not bad, kid." You don't hear the coach reciting, "What is an Athlete?" – by Flora Framble Frickard.

So you figure, why can't you find a Mother's Day card that says it simply: "Not bad, Ma." "Nice going." "'Preciate it."

Well, you can. That's the point, you see. They are all over the place. They're the cards that get handled twenty times, the ones that set your innards congealing. Funny thing, but the sappiest card turns out to be the one that tries to say it simply -- without sentiment. It's the card you hand to Mom as you go out the door. "Oh, I almost forgot to give you this."

I've figured something out. It's not sweetness that cloys; it's artificial sweetness. And there's nothing quite so artificial as trying to toss off your feelings for Mom in a catchy phrase. It embarrasses both parties. And it's a great shame, because there are cards around that won't embarrass Mom in the slightest.

This hit me the other day while I was rummaging for something in the attic. I turned up a packet of Mother's Day cards my wife has saved up over the years. There was a frilly creation, old and faded, right on the top.

"What is a Mom?" this card asks, and amidst flowers and bluebirds, it expands at length. Here and there, a glowing adjective is circled in coloring pencil. And at the end of the verse, there's a row of neatly-penciled kisses.

And I guess Suzanne, my step-daughter, must have looked at this card, her pencil box still warm in her hand, and worried that the sentiments might be a bit too pale, might slip past, because she drew an arrow to the right edge, luring her mom to the back, where she wrote, in four colors, I LOVE YOU, MOM.

Looking at this card, I'm thinking how natural and right the sentiments seem. It's marvelous how a kid can skirt the sticky-sweet. I guess it's the instinct kids have for saying what they really feel.

**Mom**

My mom's gone, God bless her, but if I were shopping up a Mother's Day card for her, it wouldn't take but a minute to find it.  It would be right there at the top of the rack -- the oversized one with the flowing sentiments in the fancy script -- and, yes, it would have flowers and lace.

~~~

# Morality

### Keynote Thought

*Nothing in life is so little appreciated as the moral character it takes to be a normal, everyday person.*

~~~

### Observations

*There is a final stage in the relaxation of morals where everything is offensive, but it doesn't offend anybody.*

~~~

*Two wrongs don't make a right, but some folks seem hell-bent on finding out how many wrongs will.*

~~~

*The trouble with hypocrisy is that it's so easily mistaken for a set of values.*

~~~

*To know the difference between right and wrong, one must first know the difference between wrong and different.*

~~~

*You hate to give evil a motive, seeing what it does with just opportunity.*

~~~

## Speaking For Myself

*Called to do good, I protest that I am but one person. Tempted to do evil, I reckon that one person should be sufficient.*

~~~

## Change in Strategy

*Devil, to helper: "With so-and-so, it won't be necessary to lead him astray. Just kind of follow along in his footsteps."*

~~~

# Nostalgia

*Not everything has to happen to be fondly recalled.*

~~~

## <u>Observations</u>

*Nostalgia is a process by which dreams become memories without ever having to come true.*

~~~

*Nothing is so likely to be tailored to one's needs as one's forgetfulness.*

~~~

*It's curious the way we get nostalgic for a dream that never came true, as if a dream that never came true were in the past.*

~~~

## Nostalgia

*You can get nostalgic for might-have-beens -- or you can get working on them.*

*~~~*

*Recalling days of sadness, memories haunt me. Recalling days of happiness, I haunt my memories.*

*~~~*

*Nostalgia is not so much the memory of happier days as of a time when happier days seemed right around the corner.*

*~~~*

*The mind likes to sift through memories, the heart through souvenirs.*

*~~~*

# Opportunity

## Keynote Thought

*Life is a thousand opportunities, more if that isn't enough.*

~~~

## Observations

*You do not seize an opportunity. You seize a moment and create an opportunity.*

~~~

*A question to occasionally ask yourself is what you would do if you had tomorrow to live over again.*

~~~

*It is a sad lament -- the happiness you might have found if you had taken the path that still lies there right in front of you.*

~~~

# Optimism

### Keynote Thought

*Is there any difference between optimism and the reality of a bright, sunny day?*

~~~

### Observations

*You know you're an optimist when you find yourself saying, "Okay, I know the situation is temporarily hopeless."*

~~~

*In life's poker game, the optimist sees the pessimist's night and raises him the sunrise.*

~~~

*Beethoven composed symphonies after becoming deaf. Monet painted masterpieces after going blind. A pessimist hears this and thinks, "With my luck, I'll never go deaf or blind."*

~~~

*It can be said of optimism that while sometimes mistaken, it is never sadly mistaken.*

~~~

*The pessimist observes the optimist and thinks, "All that happiness for nothing."*

~~~

*The imagination is a palette of bright colors. You can use it to touch up memories or you can use it to paint dreams.*

~~~

*A winter's tale: "Once, in a far corner of the universe , there was a small planet orbited by a sleigh and eight tiny reindeer."*

~~~

## Voice of Optimism

*"I know he's still alive, because he doesn't call and he doesn't write, which is just like him."*

~~~

# I'm An Optimist

I was thumbing through the Yellow Pages the other day, trying to find someone to replace a cracked lens in my eyeglasses. There didn't seem to be anyone. "Darn phone book," I remarked to my wife. "Town this size, and you can't find one optimist."

Joan laughed. "You don't want an optimist, silly, you want an optician -- unless you're thinking of getting rose-colored glasses."

"Yes, well, you'd think they'd have a cross-reference." I flipped a page and located "opticians," sandwiched between "ophthalmologists" and "optometrists." Without my glasses, I had to squint just to make out the headings. Leave it to the phone company not to print eyeglass listings in extra-large type.

"Are you sure I want an optician?" I asked Joan. "What about one of these other fellows -- an optometrist or an ophta...ophmatologist?"

"Ophthalmologist. No, you want an optician," Joan said.

She sounded confident, so I dialed an optician.  "How long to replace a cracked lens," I inquired.

"Two hours," a voice answered. "Maybe less. I'm an optimist."

~~~

# Parenting

*If you will plant the seed and nourish the soil,
the flower will shape itself.*

~~~

### Observations

*What makes raising a child so difficult is that
each day you have to start with the child you
have raised so far.*

~~~

*It is a parent's goal to raise an average kid who
is exceptional at everything he or she tries.*

~~~

*The most persistent false notion in parenting is
that something is happening somewhere else
that you are missing out on.*

~~~

*Raising kids is a series of mistakes that it is critical to make at the recommended age.*

~~~

*Absent from the Ten Commandments is any obligation of parent to child. We must assume that God felt it unnecessary to command by law what he had ensured by love.*

~~~

*To have a child is to realize that of all the lives you might have lived, only one was ever really possible.*

~~~

*Yes, to be a good parent, you have to make sacrifices, but that is not a requirement of parenting, it is a requirement of being good at something.*

~~~

*No matter how hard you try as a parent, you cannot apply the bandage before the bruise.*

~~~

# Passage

### Overheard at a Gravesite

*And they all said, "I'm sorry for your loss," as if you were someone who could ever be taken from me.*

~~~

### Observations

*No matter how mourned your passing, there will be a reception after the service where the chief topic of conversation will be how good the squash casserole is.*

~~~

*I've thought about living and dying, and I think it's probably better than living and being left behind.*

~~~

*If life is a stage, I wonder if when the play is over, you join the audience.*

# For Whom The Bell Tolls

*Author's Note:* In the summer of 2009, three celebrity passings came one upon another -- Ed McMahon, Farrah Fawcett and Michael Jackson. In September, a dear friend and fellow blogger, Liz Armbruster, died suddenly and unexpectedly. I wrote the following in their memory.

~~~

"Send not to know for whom the bell tolls. It tolls for thee." ~~ John Donne

~~~

*First the bell tolled for the loyal sidekick,*
*And it tolled for a perfect pace.*

*And then the bell tolled for a TV angel,*
*And it tolled for a heavenly face.*

*And then the bell tolled for the King of Pop,*
*And it tolled for an elegant grace.*

*And now the bell tolls for the lowly blogger,*
*And it tolls for the human race.*

~~~

# Perseverance

### Keynote Thought

*There are times when you just have to look in the mirror and say, "I will if you will."*

~~~

### Observations

*Let it be said of you that you had your shortcomings but being stopped by your shortcomings wasn't one of them.*

~~~

*We find in ourselves the strength to overcome every obstacle, which is a good thing, because we also find in ourselves every obstacle.*

~~~

*In the end it all comes down to what you do while you're wondering if there's any use doing it.*

~~~

*We gain no easier advantage than by relentlessly pursuing our goal while others pursue an advantage.*

~~~

*A steady everyday persistence is the quiet stream that flows at the canyon floor.*

~~~

*We think of giving up, but then we look at other people who have given up, and the results aren't that good.*

~~~

## Speaking For Myself

*I'm superstitious to this extent -- I believe that giving up before you begin is bad luck.*

~~~

## T-Shirt Slogan

*"You can say goodbye to me, but it doesn't mean I'm going anywhere."*

~~~

## Susan Boyle

*Author's Note:* In the spring of 2009 I was inspired like so many others by the unlikely success of Susan Boyle, caught so dramatically on Youtube. I wrote the following for my blog.

~~~

*Possibly we overrate Miss Boyle's accomplishment, for what has she proved but that an individual can aspire, that a cheerful perseverance can prevail, that an imprisoning mold can be cast off and that life, after all, can be fair.*

~~~

*One dream is realized, and twenty million other dreams are fetched from the closet, dusted off and tried on again for size.*

~~~

*Is it a sin to share vicariously the shining moment of another? Hardly, for the triumph of one underdog is a triumph for the species. To paraphrase the poet, Send not to know for whom the crowd cheers, it cheers for thee.*

~~~

# Pets

## Keynote Thought

*Exile a man to a desert island, allowing him only his dog, and in time his self-image will conform to his dog's opinion of him. This explains why Napoleon came back for one more shot at emperor.*

~~~

### Dry, Sly and Wry

*One thing you can learn from your dog is when to go lie under the dining room table and await developments.*

~~~

### Just An Opinion

*Every dog likes company and can be happy anywhere, but every cat would like to be an only cat in a nice clean house.*

~~~

### Speaking For Myself

*The way I look at it, my dog talks. He just has trouble enunciating.*

~~~

*I've concluded, after observation, that my Lab does not actually think, which is not to say he doesn't have an opinion.*

~~~

# Politics

## Keynote Thought

*Politics is always about what to do when common sense is a non-starter.*

~~~

## Observations

*No political party has a monopoly on truth, in the same way that no lynch mob has a monopoly on justice.*

~~~

*There is nothing more pointless than a political party that can't get its lie together.*

~~~

*The ultimate test of majority rule is its willingness to educate the minority's kids.*

~~~

### Speaking For Myself

*Don't know about you, but whenever I hear a politician say, "The party's over," I wonder just where exactly was this so-called party.*

~~~

*A question I always ask myself before voting is this, "Would I ever want to find myself at this person's mercy?"*

~~~

### Dry, Sly and Wry

*It is a persistent delusion that electing someone to political office will get them to go away.*

~~~

*A conservative is someone who as a child thought the  monster in the closet was in the country illegally.*

~~~

# Pretending

## Keynote Thought

*Looking back on our lives, we invariably find that the person we pretended to be is the person we became.*

~~~

## Observations

*It doesn't matter that you pretend, provided you're the person you pretend to be when people are counting on it.*

~~~

*We pretend so that we might be loved and then complain that we are not loved for who we are.*

~~~

*There are days when you think, "I should stop pretending," but then you think "No, that wouldn't be who I am."*

~~~

# Quality of Life

*Let not the perfect be the enemy of the good.*
*Let not the good be the enemy of the mediocre.*
*Let not the mediocre be the enemy of the*
*perfectly dreadful.*

*And down the slippery slope we go.*

~~~

## Observations

*The problem with settling for "good enough" is that it's so hard to distinguish it from "almost good enough."*

~~~

*If you don't recognize quality when you encounter it, your life tends to shape itself so that you never encounter it.*

~~~

*Where you find quality, you will find a craftsman, not a quality control expert.*

~~~

*Most of the excellence we see in the world is the product not of talent or genius but of self-respect.*

~~~

*Always, where you find a work of excellence, you find some individual's name attached to it.*

~~~

# Reality

### Keynote Thought

*I don't deny reality, but I don't exactly go looking for it, either.*

~~~

### Observations

*Reject the evidence of your eyes long enough, and they eventually give up and start seeing what you want them to see.*

~~~

*You can accept reality, or you can hold fast to your dream and force reality to accept you.*

~~~

*You wonder if the Creator of reality ever guessed that people would take it so literally.*

~~~

*There's fact, and there's fiction, which is a good thing because it's hard to explain anything using just one.*

~~~

*It is said that all is illusion, but as long as there is an illusion that the kids need to be fed, all might as well be reality.*

~~~

## Speaking For Myself

*I may accept reality, but it does not imply endorsement.*

~~~

*I've never thought it my business to disturb anyone who lives in an alternative world in which they get along just fine.*

~~~

*Seems like nothing ever brings you back to reality that makes you want to stay there.*

~~~

**Reality**

*I have learned over the years that my eyes can construct a figment as easily as my imagination.*

*~~~*

*If I believe in God, it is because I have seen reality, and I just can't believe it is non-negotiable.*

*~~~*

### Dry, Sly and Wry

*To accept reality is only to encourage it.*

*~~~*

*Reality is not some fantasy world we imagine. It is a world of demonstrable fact we imagine.*

*~~~*

*You can accept reality without believing every yarn it spins.*

*~~~*

# Reconciliation

## Keynote Thought

*Eventually you realize that nothing that benefits you and you alone benefits anyone.*

~~~

## Observations

*Sometimes two people just need to return to some old fork in the road and, together, take the other path.*

~~~

*Often a tug o' war is better than not connecting at all.*

~~~

*It is a shame to separate from the right companion because you are on the wrong journey.*

~~~

**Reconciliation**

*You can't just wish away the people in your life and start over again, but sometimes you can all start over again.*

*~~~*

*There are times when two people need to step apart from one another, but there is no rule that says they have to turn and fire.*

*~~~*

# Relationships

### Keynote Thought

*No matter how passionate the relationship, it is sustained in the end by its everyday courtesies.*

~~~

### Observations

*The saddest thing in a relationship is trying to make it last by never letting it begin.*

~~~

*In every relationship there are situations you need to talk through -- and situations where you need to be through talking.*

~~~

*Occasionally it's good to tell someone you love exactly what you would tell them if they had just died in your arms.*

~~~

*No relationship can last that demands more of both parties than it provides to either.*

~~~

*A truce is not a relationship, and if you're the only one observing it, it's not a truce, either.*

~~~

*The way to make a good relationship better is to appreciate it just the way it is.*

~~~

*As hard as you try, it is impossible to travel diverging paths and still meet back every night in the same place.*

~~~

*In a relationship, the rule, "If it ain't broke, don't fix it," is a good reason to break it every now and then.*

~~~

*To stay in a relationship rather than hurt your partner may not be love, but it usually seems that way to an outside observer.*

~~~

*To some, it is love undeniably.  To others, it is making it work, whatever it is.*

~~~

*No relationship is as strong as it can be until it has survived the thing most likely to destroy it.*

~~~

*Sometimes you know a relationship won't work but you enter it anyway, because it would be so cool it if did.*

~~~

*We all know them -- two people who could never part without a kiss.  But now they never part, and so never kiss.*

~~~

*You can't owe loyalty to someone to whom you owe nothing else.*

~~~

*It is never wise to enter a partnership for the purpose of gaining an advantage over your partner.*

~~~

*Sadly, relationships end, a reason to always keep on hand a bottle of champagne and two glasses.*

~~~

*It's sad to see a relationship unravel, but it's probably better than a surprise ending.*

~~~

## If You Want My Advice

*This morning, smile at a stranger. I mean, before you say, "Pass the toast."*

~~~

*Beware a relationship where the only thing you have in common is a low opinion of someone else.*

~~~

## A Novel in One Line

*Once there were two people who always agreed on the hardest way to do everything --and they lived happily ever after.*

~~~

# Responsibility

*At some point you must decide if you want to succeed or just be someone who was never to blame for anything going wrong.*

~~~

## Observations

*Never start taking the blame for others with the idea that you will be notified when you can stop.*

~~~

*When there is hell to pay, it is usually cheaper to pay it than to finance an endless purgatory.*

~~~

*As a rule of thumb, the higher your position of responsibility, the more likely you never have to take responsibility for anything.*

~~~

## Dry, Sly and Wry

*I always figure it's somebody else's fault.  After all, there is only one me and seven billion somebody elses.  I mean, like, duh!*

~~~

*Next time my analyst says, "If you're unhappy, you know who to blame, don't you?" -- I got a list of names in my hip pocket.*

~~~

*The concept of Original Sin is proof that it is never too late to blame yourself for everything that ever happened.*

~~~

# Sanity

*Madness is defined in different ways at different times, sanity being the ability to keep up with the changes.*

~~~

### <u>Observations</u>

*There is no sane person who does not at times deny reality in order to stay sane.*

~~~

*Sanity is the ability to put things out of your mind before they drive you there.*

~~~

*What the insane basically lack is the willingness to accept some preposterous notion that makes sense of everything else.*

~~~

### Dry, Sly and Wry

*Analyst to patient: "Would you say you're in a state of denial?"*

*Patient: No, I deny everything pretty much as it comes up."*

~~~

*paranoia: the belief that everyone is out to get you.*

*neurosis: the belief that everyone is out to give you back.*

~~~

# Skepticism

## Keynote Thought

*The skeptic sees God revealed in nature and doubts Him, sees God revealed in Scripture and doubts Him, sees God revealed in the worship of countless believers and doubts Him, sees God revealed even as the object of his own doubt -- and doubts Him. The skeptic has no wish to believe, for he finds in doubt a religion absolved of any requirement to prove itself, an anti-faith whose god reveals himself nowhere -- not in nature, not in scripture, not in the worship of the mass of mankind. How clever it is of skepticism, having no evidence to offer in its own support, to pose as doubt.*

~~~

## The Skeptic

*I live in a world where events have no cause and phenomena no origin. I reject the self-evident because it cannot be proved by the suspect. I acknowledge that I know nothing, yet reject all that I do not know. I am a skeptic. Welcome, Alice, to my strange land.*

~~~

## Observations

*You must realize that skepticism, too, is a religion, albeit a religion very rich in evangelists and very short on saviors.*

~~~

*Of what use to understand the nuances of everything and the essence of nothing?*

~~~

*I respect more the person doubtful of his faith than the person confident in his doubt.*

~~~

# Social Networking

*The great thing about social networking is that you get to meet people you otherwise would only meet if you were committed to the same asylum.*

~~~

## Observations

*Some say the world will end by fire, some say by ice, some say by the simultaneous crash of Instagram and Facebook.*

~~~

*A social networker is an average person who happens to have a need to count his or her friends every half hour.*

~~~

*One thing social networking has made possible is the application of mob psychology without having to assemble a mob.*

~~~

*The problem is, if you're not into social networking, people think you're anti-social when you're only anti-networking.*

~~~

## The Blogosphere

*A blog is a message in a bottle, both in purpose and likely readership.*

~~~

*A blog seems to have two magnetic poles, one attracting friends, the other repulsing relatives.*

~~~

*A blogger is someone constantly looking over his shoulder, for fear that he is not being followed.*

~~~

# The Social Scene

### Keynote Thought

*Nothing about you will mean less to posterity than whether you gained social acceptance in your lifetime.*

~~~

### Observations

*Society is forever trying to convince us that there are certain obligations we agreed to when we volunteered to be born.*

~~~

*It is always those who have already won the game who decide that now it ought to have rules.*

~~~

*A pleasant smile is the wisest comment, always interpreted favorably and rarely misquoted.*

~~~

✧

*You can be sure that the person who disparages others in your presence disparages you in their presence.*

~~~

## Speaking For Myself

*I like to think that I have achieved a certain social status. I mean, "misfit" is a status, isn't it?*

~~~

*I don't look at it as being ignored. I look at it as another day of successfully avoiding the paparazzi.*

~~~

*Ah, yes, my social life -- a series of encounters where we briefly debate who is in the greater rush.*

~~~

*I not only believe in the unconscious mind, it keeps most of my social engagements.*

~~~

# Sorrow

*What sorrow does not linger in memory as an ever sweeter sadness?*

~~~

## Observations

*The sorrow of loss is an inseparable part of happiness, all one experience to be accepted in its every stage.*

~~~

*Sorrow differs from happiness in that it is recognizable while in progress.*

~~~

*You can avoid most of life's sorrows, the only requirement being that you avoid all of its happiness.*

~~~

# Soulmates

*A soulmate is someone who knows where you
went when you were last seen wandering
aimlessly.*

~~~

### Observations

*Sometimes two people meet who have no
illusions -- and discover they are ready for one.*

~~~

*There is no motivation like a world that thinks
you can't and a partner who thinks you can.*

~~~

*You can be happy with someone who likes you
despite your faults -- until you meet someone
who likes your faults.*

~~~

*Sometimes it's worth getting lost to see who will come looking for us.*

~~~

*You can usually recognize soulmates. In a noisy singles bar, they will be the two people listening to the band.*

~~~

*If there be a Judgment Day, the Lord's principal dilemma will be how to judge two people who have shared one soul.*

~~~

## Speaking For Myself

*Born to loving parents and grandparents, we grow up thinking that the world is full of people who will place our happiness above their own. We discover, if we are lucky in life, that there is exactly one more.*

~~~

# Success

### Keynote Thought

*Show up, work hard, learn from your mistakes,
and in the end it will all seem like a strategy.*

~~~

### Observations

*It can be said of most successful people that they
would have settled for less, but no one ever
offered them less.*

~~~

*The trick to getting ahead is to give it the same
effort you give to getting even.*

~~~

*If there's one thing that you and you alone are
the final judge of, it is whether or not you are a
success.*

~~~

*What you discover about people who have all that life offers is that they didn't wait for it to be offered.*

~~~

*It might be instructive, occasionally, to pretend you're accepting an award for failure, just to see who you would thank.*

~~~

*As a jobseeker, remember this -- you only lack experience if they want it done the same old way.*

~~~

*How do you achieve success? Well, for one thing, you don't define it before you achieve it.*

~~~

*You don't take over a room by making everyone in it feel small. You take over a room by making everyone in it feel noticed.*

~~~

### If You Want My Advice

*Never envy another person's success unless you can recall envying their struggle.*

~~~

### Dry. Sly and Wry

*Every success you have in life is just something else for your mom to worry about.*

~~~

*Failure is the insufficient foresight to have a fuzzy enough goal.*

~~~

*We all make mistakes. The trick is to make your mistakes big enough so that they don't seem like only one person's fault.*

~~~

*Meanwhile, sales of my book, "How To Succeed By Working Your Tail Off" have reached single digits.*

~~~

# Thanksgiving

~~~

*"Lord, we gather as a family to thank Thee for all Thy blessings, most especially for making us this family and granting us this gathering."*

~~~

## Thanksgiving At Our House

This year we tossed a coin, and the kids will sit at the dining room table and the adults at the card table in the living room.

A secret I will take to the grave is how I carve the dark meat in slices and the white meat in chunks.

My wife says that this year she'll carve the turkey and I can carve the gelatin mold.

You can be humbled by praise, or you can be humbled by carrying in the turkey and having it slide off the platter into your mother-in-law's lap.

This year we're having the words. "There's more gravy in the kitchen" stitched right on the napkins.

As customary, we've designated Aunt Viv to say grace and Uncle Howie to say "Let's eat."

At our house we have a rule that the cook has to come to the table so we can all get started, then she can go back to the kitchen.

As usual, we've invited an odd number of people, so there won't be a tie vote on whether to have the pies right after dinner or wait an hour.

As always, the pie-serving honors will go to Cousin Marian, who cuts the biggest slivers.

Speaking for myself, when I ask for a sliver of mince pie, I do mean a sliver.

I suppose I will die never knowing what pumpkin pie tastes like when you have room for it.

~~~

# Time and Mortality

### Keynote Thought

*We are all time-sharers on planet Earth. We are not asked to leave it a better place. We are merely asked not to break the furniture or stain the rug.*

~~~

## Observations

*Another day, another chance to travel into tomorrow's past and change it.*

~~~

*One day, in your busy life, there's a knock on the  door and a voice says, "Come, I will show you where the time went."*

~~~

*Nothing lasts forever, although we often underestimate how long it will last in the meantime.*

~~~

*To apply what-ifs to the past and so-be-its to the future is to get it exactly backwards.*

~~~

*The miracle of the loaves and fishes is nothing compared to the miracle of the 24 hours, which the Lord distributes each day among the multitude such that each gets the whole 24.*

~~~

## Dry, Sly and Wry

*You'll know that time is traveling backwards when something that's annoying becomes cute.*

~~~

*Time heals everything, although not so much a highway bridge built in 1936.*

~~~

## Speaking For Myself

*Of all the ways I can think of to achieve immortality, living forever seems the least useful to anybody.*

~~~

*I would rather be mortal and know that death is inescapable than be immortal and know that life is inescapable.*

~~~

# Trust

*For every grown-up you can trust, there was first a child who was trusted.*

~~~

## Observations

*People will sometimes let you down, but it is a risky plan that assumes they will.*

~~~

*Give your trust freely, and you will find that those who would not lift a finger to earn it will work their tail off to keep it.*

~~~

*You cannot teach your kids not to trust anyone and expect they will make an exception of you.*

~~~

# Truth and Lies

### Keynote Thought

*It is a shame to never admit the truth to yourself and wonder forever if you might have been able to handle it.*

*~~~*

### Observations

*It is possible to know the truth about someone and not be the person they need to hear it from.*

*~~~*

*There are more martyrs to nonsense than truth, truth preferring missionaries.*

*~~~*

*A clever liar always underestimates the cleverness of the truth.*

*~~~*

*It is possible to love a liar -- and just kind of hope that you never hear the words, "I love you."*

~~~

*Sometimes it isn't a lie; it is just the truth broken very gently.*

~~~

## Dry, Sly and Wry

*Know what's fun? Find someone who can't handle the truth, and just keep telling it to them.*

~~~

*Overheard: "There's not a deceitful bone in his body, but look out for his vocal chords."*

~~~

## If You Want My Advice

*Whatever you plan to do when everybody finds out the truth, get ready to do right now.*

~~~

## The Kind Lie Vs The Unkind Truth

I did not suppose, when I wrote the following line, that I was saying anything especially controversial:

*"Today I bent the truth to be kind, and I have no regret, for I am far surer of what is kind than I am of what is true."*

-- or when I reiterated the view in this line:

*"When a friend needs consolation, nothing will keep so well until tomorrow as the truth."*

But twice I have seen the first line debated in internet chatrooms, the verdict each time being that telling a falsehood is always bad, opening a Pandora's Box to all manner of disaster. How do I respond to this? I respond by coming down coming squarely on the side of kindness. I believe this puts me on the side of the God of both testaments of the Judaeo-Christian tradition, – the God who gave us the Ten Commandments and the God who gave us the Sermon on the Mount.

To my ear, the commandment against lying seems to have been carefully crafted to exclude the lie of kind intent: "Thou shalt not bear false witness against thy neighbor." The God of Moses had no trouble with clarity. He was explicit in saying "Thou shalt not kill" and "Thou shalt not steal," these being clear assaults against one's neighbor. But had He said, "Thou shalt not lie," his law might have been construed to condone an assault of truth against one's neighbor. Instead, His commandment puts the emphasis clearly on the consideration of our neighbor's welfare. The short form of the commandment is not "Thou shalt not lie" but "Thou shalt not harm thy neighbor by thy word." It is a corollary to "Love thy neighbor as thyself."

In the Sermon on the Mount, Christ spoke of those "who say all manner of evil against you falsely." He did not condemn those who say all manner of good of you, in the interest of your welfare, be it false or otherwise. Here is the God who reduced the commandments to two: Love thy God and Love thy neighbor. In giving us the beatitude, "Blessed are the merciful...," did He intend to exclude from the merciful those who bend the truth so as not to hurt their neighbor?

I think of it this way – there is a distinction between the facts that we discern as truth, and the Eternal Truth which is God Himself, to whom our only allegiance is owed, and who has provided us the model of kindness and understanding that should inform our lives. And so, for myself at least, the rule is simple:

*"Love thy neighbor, and if it requires that you bend your understanding of the truth, the Truth will understand."*

~~~

# Vacations

### Keynote Thought

*While I don't wish to idle away my life, I do wish to idle away the portion of it intended for that purpose.*

~~~

### Observations

*There are times when you seek respite from your life, only to find yourself calling every hour to check on it.*

~~~

*If you're a dad or mom, here's a question for you -- when was the last time you had a vacation, just the two of you, not counting guilt trips?*

~~~

## Oh, Those Vacation Photos

My wife and I have just returned from a family vacation, and we have some wonderful photos.

Actually, the ones of me are awful, but the ones of everyone else are great. My wife says that the ones of her are awful, but the ones of me are great. Her mother, who vacationed with us, called up to say that she has some great photos – except for the ones of her, which are awful. Our daughter called to say that she has clipped herself out of all her photos. They're awful, she says -- but she has some great ones of the rest of us.

It's funny how everyone thinks the photos of themselves are awful, and the photos of everyone else are great. It's probably because we think we look so goofy in the photos, when to everyone else, that's the way we always look.

That's the thing about vacation photos – everyone looks just the way they always do, except you. You look like someone who got up in the middle of the night to go to the bathroom and wandered into the photograph.

How many times have you looked at a photo of yourself, thinking you might slip it under the couch cushion, when someone looks over your shoulder and says, "That's great of you." That's what people do – they look at a photo of you that might have been taken by the coroner's office, and say, "You look good in that." Makes you want to find a really rotten photo of them and say, "That is sooooo good of you." But you can't find a rotten photo of them. They all look great.

Personally, I have this thing in group photos where I'm the only one saying cheese. Everyone else has a broad happy smile on their face, or else they're poking each other and giggling, or mugging for the camera. And I'm standing there saying cheese.

Our neighbors just vacationed with their kids, and they have some great photos. There's one of their 6-year old standing on the beach, next to a giant sand castle, looking proud as can be. I said to him, "That's a great photo of you." He looked at the photo and screwed up his face. "That is actually sick," he said.

~~~

# Wall Street

### Keynote Thought

*Wall Street greed is growing by leaps. There are no bounds.*

~~~

### Observations

*If you think that someone's plotting to steal everything you have, you're either paranoid or a member of the middle class.*

~~~

*I don't know how the world will end, but I suspect it will coincide with the highest corporate profits ever recorded.*

~~~

*If bankers were astronomers, every sunrise would be an event that no one could have seen coming.*

~~~

# War

### Keynote Thought

*There is no excuse for war so cynical that it won't seem noble after the first soldier has died for it.*

~~~

### Observations

*The problem with a country defending its honor is that it always defends more honor than it has.*

~~~

*Man, in his sensitivity, does not give names to animals he intends to slaughter but goes on giving names to children he intends to send to war.*

~~~

*The only lesson any general ever learned from war is not to invade Russia in summer uniform.*

~~~

# Women

### Keynote Thought

*As long as there are women in the world, men will have an exaggerated idea of how many things take care of themselves.*

~~~

### Observations

*A man finds love and is satisfied. A woman finds love and insists on turning it into happiness.*

~~~

*A man sometimes win an argument, but a woman always wins a silence.*

~~~

*No woman is so confined to her destiny that she won't find a way to pick the color scheme.*

~~~

*One of the great logical puzzles is how every woman is just like her mother but nothing like her sister.*

~~~

*The first job of motherhood is to get a child safely to the point where its father is ready for fatherhood.*

~~~

*There is an instinct in a woman to love most her own child -- and an instinct to make any child who needs her love, her own.*

~~~

~~~

# Appendix

~~~

# Potpourri

*Overheard at a wake: "Thank God she didn't live to see what the mortician did with her hair."*

*~~~*

*The explanation is always longer when there isn't any.*

*~~~*

*Don't know about yours, but my psychoanalyst charges only $25 a session, and he not only gives advice, he cuts hair.*

*~~~*

*People say to you, "What good will worrying do?", as if you were worrying for the good it will do.*

*~~~*

*Sometimes, opportunities are missed, as when the priest, the rabbi and the minister make it to the lifeboat, but the jokewriter drowns.*

*~~~*

## Potpourri

Most people would rather defend to the death
your right to say it than listen to it.

~~~

There's a whole list of scams I might fall for -- if
I knew how to wire money to Nigeria.

~~~

One thing all religions agree on is that after six
days of breakfast, lunch and dinner, there
should be one day of brunch and supper.

~~~

Sign over the gates of hell: "Doesn't mean
you're a bad person."

~~~

A speedreader has already finished this book
and gone to lunch. But you are only here. And
now you're here. You see the problem?

~~~

Sign over the gates of hell: "Immediate delivery
anywhere in the world."

~~~

*You know it's a nasty divorce when they can't agree on how to divvy up the His and Hers towels.*

~~~

*Ever wonder what crime you committed that you are confined to a small enclosure above your sinuses under permanent skull arrest?*

~~~

*My health plan doesn't cover dental, so I enrolled my teeth as 32 dependents, each needing a complete yearly physical.*

~~~

*The object of most prayers is to wangle an advance on good intentions.*

~~~

*The trouble with having a physical body is that people know it's where you hang out, and you don't get any privacy.*

~~~

*It never fails. Whenever I'm asked to name the Seven Wharfs, I always forget Dock.*

**Potpourri**

*Classified Ad: Bundle of good intentions seeks mindreader.*

*~~~*

*Overheard: "I see in myself a little bit of St. Francis. I mean, assuming I were to give away my possessions and start helping the poor."*

*~~~*

*The frustrating thing about reading "The Lives of the Saints" is that just when it gets interesting, they change their ways.*

*~~~*

*It is not gossip when there is absolutely no other way to bring up the subject.*

*~~~*

*And God said, "Be fruitful and multiply," whereupon He created the moon, saying, "Let there be indirect lighting."*

*~~~*

96010895R00121

Made in the USA
Columbia, SC
19 May 2018